The Pegan Diet Cookbook

Little Known Pegan Recipes to Cook Like a Chef and Experience Immense Health Benefits… Without Odd Ingredients!

Ruby-Rose Mcnally

Cuisine Cook Publishing

CONTENTS

DRINKS & SMOOTHIES

Coconut Milk Pineapple Smoothie

Preparation Time: 10 minutes | Cook time: 0 minutes | Servings 2

1/2 cup chopped dandelion greens

1/2 cup arugula

2 cups chopped pineapple

1 medium banana, peeled

1 cup water

1 cup canned full-fat coconut milk, divided

1 Place dandelion greens, arugula, and pineapple, banana, water and 1/2 cup coconut milk in a blender and blend until thoroughly combined.

2 Add remaining coconut milk while blending until desired texture is achieved.

Nutrition Facts

Calorie 315| Fat 17g| Carbs 38g| Protein 3g

Chocolate Oatmeal Banana Smoothie

Preparation Time: 10 minutes | Cook time: 0 minutes | Servings 2

1 cup chopped romaine lettuce

2 medium bananas, peeled

1 tablespoon cocoa powder

1/2 teaspoon vanilla bean pulp

2 cups oat milk, divided

1 Place romaine, bananas, cocoa powder, vanilla bean pulp, and 1 cup oat milk in a blender and blend until thoroughly combined.

2 Add remaining oat milk while blending until desired texture is achieved.

Nutrition Facts

Calorie 230| Fat 3g| Carbs 49g| Protein 7g

Healthy Peach Coconut Smoothie

Preparation Time: 10 minutes | Cook time: 0 minutes | Servings 2

1 large orange, peeled

1 medium peach, pitted

1 medium banana, peeled

1 Watercress

1 cup canned full-fat coconut milk, divided

1 Place watercress, orange, peach, banana, and 1/2 cup coconut milk in a blender and blend until thoroughly combined.

2 Add remaining coconut milk while blending until desired texture is achieved.

Nutrition Facts

Calorie 300| Fat 15g| Carbs 33g| Protein 4g

Apple Banana Protein Smoothie

Preparation Time: 10 minutes | Cook time: 0 minutes | Servings 2

2 cups spinach

1 medium banana, peeled

2 medium apples, cored and peeled

2 cups unsweetened vanilla almond milk, divided

1 Place spinach, banana, apples, and 1 cup almond milk in a blender and blend until thoroughly combined.

2 Add remaining almond milk while blending until desired texture is achieved.

Nutrition Facts

Calorie 183| Fat 3g| Carbs 39g| Protein 3g

Tasty Raspberry Mango Smoothie

Preparation Time: 10 minutes | Cook time: 0 minutes | Servings 2

1 cup chopped watercress

1 medium mango, pitted and peeled

1 cup raspberries

11/2 cups oat milk, divided

1 Place watercress, mango, raspberries, and 3/4 cup oat milk in a blender and blend until thoroughly combined.

2 Add remaining oat milk while blending until desired texture is achieved.

Nutrition Facts

Calorie 232| Fat 3g| Carbs 50g| Protein 6g

Fresh Green Smoothie

Preparation Time: 10 minutes | Cook time: 0 minutes | Servings 1

1 cup chopped romaine lettuce

2 medium cucumbers, peeled and quartered

1/4 cup chopped mint

1 cup water, divided

1 Place romaine, cucumbers, mint, and 1/2 cup water in a blender and combine thoroughly.

2 Add remaining water while blending until desired texture is achieved.

Nutrition Facts

Calorie 40| Fat 0g| Carbs 9g| Protein 2g

Almond Milk Cherry Smoothie

Preparation Time: 10 minutes | Cook time: 0 minutes | Servings 2

1 cup chopped iceberg lettuce

2 medium pears, cored

1 medium banana, peeled

1/2 cup pitted cherries

1/2 teaspoon vanilla bean pulp

2 cups unsweetened vanilla almond milk, divided

1 Place lettuce, pears, banana, cherries, vanilla bean pulp, and 1 cup almond milk in a blender and blend until thoroughly combined.

2 Add remaining almond milk while blending until desired texture is achieved.

Nutrition Facts

Calorie 216| Fat 3g| Carbs 48g| Protein 3g

Homemade Oats Apple Smoothie

Preparation Time: 10 minutes | Cook time: 0 minutes | Servings 2

2 tablespoons rolled oats

1 cup chopped watercress

2 medium peaches, pitted

2 medium apples, cored and peeled

cups unsweetened vanilla almond milk, divided

1. Place oats, watercress, peaches, apples, and 1 cup almond milk in a blender and blend until thoroughly combined.

2. Add remaining almond milk while blending until desired texture is achieved.

Nutrition Facts

Calorie 198| Fat 4g| Carbs 43g| Protein 4g

Spinach Zucchini Smoothie

Preparation Time: 10 minutes | Cook time: 0 minutes | Servings 2

1 cup spinach

1 medium zucchini, chopped

3 medium carrots, peeled and chopped

2 medium apples, cored and peeled

2 cups water, divided

1 Place spinach, zucchini, carrots, apples, and 1 cup water in a blender and blend until thoroughly combined.

2 Add remaining water while blending until desired texture is achieved.

Nutrition Facts

Calorie 163| Fat 1g| Carbs 40g| Protein 4g

Broccoli Zucchini Smoothie

Preparation Time: 10 minutes | Cook time: 0 minutes | Servings 2

1 cup chopped romaine lettuce

1 cup chopped broccoli

1 medium zucchini, chopped

2 medium carrots, peeled and chopped

2 cups water, divided

1 Place romaine, broccoli, zucchini, carrots, and 1 cup water in a blender and blend until thoroughly combined.

2 Add remaining water while blending until desired texture is achieved.

Nutrition Facts

Calorie 71| Fat 1g| Carbs 15g| Protein 4g

Cranberry Cocktail Recipe

Preparation Time: 10 minutes | Cook time: 0 minutes | Servings 2

¼ cup cranberry juice cocktail

2/3 cup silken tofu, firm

½ cup raspberries, frozen, unsweetened

½ cup blueberries, frozen, unsweetened

1 teaspoon vanilla extract

1 Pour juice into a blender. Add rest of ingredients. Blend until very smooth.

2 Serve immediately and enjoy!

Nutrition Facts

Calorie 440| Fat 3.8g| Carbs 95.24g| Protein 8.04g

Banana Yogurt-Oat bran Smoothie

Preparation Time: 10 minutes | Cook time: 0 minutes | Servings 2

½ banana, peeled and cut into chunks

½ cup plain yogurt

½ cup applesauce, unsweetened

¼ cup almond or rice milk

1 tablespoon honey

2 tablespoons oat or wheat bran

1. Place banana, yogurt, applesauce, milk and honey in blender.

2. Blend until smooth.

3. Add oat bran and blend until thickened.

Nutrition Facts

Calorie 236| Fat 5.62g| Carbs 44.4g| Protein 7.67g

Healthy Spicy Cranberry- Dates Juice

Preparation Time: 10 minutes | Cook time: 0 minutes | Servings 2

1 cup organic cranberries

4 cups of filtered water, divided

4 dates or 2 Tablespoon date paste or 2 Tablespoon maple syrup

2 red organic apples, sliced

Juice of 2 organic lemons

1 Teaspoon Cardamom (optional)

1 sprig fresh organic mint or peppermint (optional)

1 In a medium size pot combines the cranberries and 3 cups of water and brings to a boil.

2 Turn the heat off and let cool. In a food processor blend the dates or date paste with lemon juice and remaining one cup of water.

3 Transfer to a large glass container or jar and add sliced apples, and all the cranberries and water.

4 Stir and add cardamom and mint leaves if desired.

Nutrition Facts

Calorie 622| Fat 1.51g| Carbs 155.45g| Protein 1.73g

Vanilla Whey Protein Drink

Preparation Time: 10 minutes | Cook time: 0 minutes | Servings 2

3/4 cup pineapple sherbet or sorbet

1 scoop vanilla whey protein powder

1/2 cup water

2 ice cubes, optional

1 In a blender, add pineapple sherbet, whey protein powder and water (ice cubes optional).

2 Immediately blend for 30 to 45 seconds.

Nutrition Facts

Calorie 215| Fat 0.48g| Carbs 37.67g| Protein 17.47g

Strawberry- Pomegranate Smoothie

Preparation Time: 10 minutes | Cook time: 30 minutes | Servings 2

1¼ mugs unsweetened coconut milk or almond milk

¼ mug unsweetened pomegranate juice

¼ mug unable salted almond butter

1 moderate red beet, peeled and quartered (about 4 ounces)

2½ mugs hulled fresh strawberries

1½ mugs frozen unsweetened mango chunks

2 teaspoons egg white grinding grains

1 In a moderate sauce dish prepare beet, Wrap upped, in a small amount of boiling water for 30 minutes or until very tender.

2 Drain beet; run cold water over beet to cool quickly and drain well.

3 In a blender combine beet, strawberries, mango chunks, coconut milk, pomegranate juice, and almond butter.

4 Wrap up and blend until smooth, stopping to scrape sides of blender as needed. Insert egg white grinding grains.

5 Wrap up and blend just until combined. Shift frozen mango pieces to an airtight container; freeze for up to 3 months.

Nutrition Facts

Calorie 50| Fat 0.25g| Carbs 10.22g| Protein 2.62g

Classic Almond Banana Date Shake

Preparation Time: 15 minutes | Cook time: 0 minutes | Servings 2

2 Tablespoon almond butter

1 tablespoon egg white grinding grains

1 tablespoon unsweetened cocoa grinding grains (optional)

½ Teaspoon. fresh lemon juice

⅓ Mug sliced off, pitted Medjool dates

1 mug unsweetened almond or coconut milk (with vanilla if desired)

1 ripe banana, frozen and sliced

⅛ Teaspoon ground nutmeg

1 In a small pot combine date and ½ mug water.

2 Microwave on immense for 30 seconds or until dates are softened; drain off water.

3 In a blender combine the dates, almond milk, banana slices, almond butter, egg white grinding grains, cocoa grinding grains (if using), lemon juice, and nutmeg.

4 Wrap up and blend until smooth.

Nutrition Facts

Calorie 247| Fat 23.9g| Carbs 9.52g| Protein3.04g

Apple Tea for Weight loss

Preparation Time: 15 minutes | Cook time: 5 minutes | Servings 2

1 cup unsweetened rice milk

1 chai tea bag

1 apple, peeled, cored, and chopped

2 cups ice

1 In a medium saucepan, heat the rice milk over low heat for about 5 minutes or until steaming.

2 Remove the milk from the heat and add the tea bag to steep.

3 Let the milk cool in the refrigerator with the tea bag for about 20 minutes and then remove tea bag, squeezing gently to release the entire flavor.

4 Place the milk, apple, and ice in a blender and blend until smooth.

5 Pour into 2 glasses and serve.

Nutrition Facts

Calorie 243| Fat 8.29g| Carbs g| Protein 8.16g

Blueberry Pineapple Smoothie

Preparation Time: 15 minutes | Cook time: 0 minutes | Servings 2

1 cup frozen blueberries

½ cup pineapple chunks

½ cup English cucumber

½ apples

½ cup water

1 Put the blueberries, pineapple, cucumber, apple, and water in a blender and

2 Blend until thick and smooth.

3 Pour into 2 glasses and serve.

Nutrition Facts

Calorie 239| Fat 1.36g| Carbs 59.91g| Protein 1.73g

Watermelon Raspberry Smoothie

Preparation Time: 15 minutes | Cook time: 0 minutes | Servings 2

½ cup boiled, cooled, and shredded red cabbage

1 cup diced watermelon

½ cup fresh raspberries

1 cup ice

1 Put the cabbage in a blender and pulse for 2 minutes or until it is finely chopped.

2 Add the watermelon and raspberries and pulse for about 1 minute or until very well combined.

3 Add the ice and blend until the smoothie is very thick and smooth.

4 Pour into 2 glasses and serve.

Nutrition Facts

Calorie 176| Fat 0.46g| Carbs 44.81g| Protein 2.64g

Chilled and Creamy Berry Dessert

Preparation Time: 15 minutes | Cook time: 10 minutes | Servings 2

1 cup vanilla rice milk, at room temperature

½ cup plain cream cheese, at room temperature

1 tablespoon granulated sugar

½ teaspoon ground cinnamon

1 cup crumbled Meringue Cookies

2 cups fresh blueberries

1 cup sliced fresh strawberries

1 In a small bowl, whisk together the milk, cream cheese, sugar, and cinnamon until smooth.

2 Into 4 (6-ounce) glasses, spoon ¼ cup of crumbled cookie in the bottom of each.

3 Spoon ¼ cup of the cream cheese mixture on top of the cookies.

4 Top the cream cheese with ¼ cup of the berries.

5 Repeat in each cup with the cookies, cream cheese mixture, and berries.

6 Chill in the refrigerator for 1 hour and serve.

Nutrition Facts

Calorie 1624| Fat 59.25g| Carbs 258.99g| Protein 29.03g

Homemade Vanilla Hot Cereal

Preparation Time: 15 minutes | Cook time: 10 minutes | Servings 2

2¼ cups water

1¼ cups vanilla rice milk

6 tablespoons uncooked bulgur

2 tablespoons uncooked whole buckwheat

1 cup peeled, sliced apple

6 tablespoons plain uncooked couscous

½ teaspoon ground cinnamon

1. In a medium saucepan over medium-high heat, heat the water and milk.

2. Bring to a boil, and add the bulgur, buckwheat, and apple.

3. Reduce the heat to low and simmer, stirring occasionally, for 20 to 25 minutes or until the bulgur is tender.

4. Remove the saucepan from the heat and stir in the couscous and cinnamon.

5. Let the saucepan stand, covered, for 10 minutes, and then fluff the cereal with a fork before serving.

Nutrition Facts

Calorie 476| Fat 1.89g| Carbs 105.61g| Protein 12.15g

Grandma's Tasty Corn Pudding

Preparation Time: 15 minutes | **Cook time:** 10 minutes | **Servings 2**

Unsalted butter, for greasing the baking dish

2 tablespoons all-purpose flour

½ teaspoon Ener-G baking soda substitute

3 eggs

¾ cup unsweetened rice milk, at room temperature

3 tablespoons unsalted butter, melted

2 tablespoons light sour cream

2 tablespoons granulated sugar

2 cups frozen corn kernels, thawed

1. Preheat the oven to 350°F.

2. Lightly grease an 8-by-8-inch baking dish with butter; set aside.

3. In a small bowl, stir together the flour and baking soda substitute; set aside.

4. In a medium bowl, whisk together the eggs, rice milk, butter, sour cream, and sugar.

5. Stir the flour mixture into the egg mixture until smooth.

6. Add the corn to the batter and stir until very well mixed.

7. Spoon the batter into the baking dish and bake for about 40 minutes or until the pudding is set.

8. Let the pudding cool for about 15 minutes and serve warm.

Nutrition Facts

Calorie 1358| Fat 65.11g| Carbs 142.51g| Protein 48.52g

Classic Bread Pudding

Preparation Time: 15 minutes | Cook time: 30 minutes | Servings 2

Unsalted butter, for greasing the baking dish

1½ cups unsweetened rice milk

3 eggs

½ cup granulated sugar

1 tablespoon corn-starch

1 vanilla bean, split

10 thick pieces white bread, cut into 1-inch chunks

2 cups chopped fresh rhubarb

1. Preheat the oven to 350°F.
2. Lightly grease an 8-by-8-inch baking dish with butter; set aside.
3. In a large bowl, whisk together the rice milk, eggs, sugar, and corn starch.

4. Scrape the vanilla seeds into the milk mixture and whisk to blend.

5. Add the bread to the egg mixture and stir to completely coat the bread.

6. Add the chopped rhubarb and stir to combine.

7. Let the bread and egg mixture soak for 5 minutes.

8. Spoon the mixture into the prepared baking dish, cover with aluminum foil, and bake for 20 minutes.

9. Uncover the bread pudding and bake for an additional 10 minutes or until the pudding is golden brown and set.

10. Serve warm.

Nutrition Facts

Calorie 1605| Fat 35.89g| Carbs 285.77g| Protein 45.03g

Onion Coconut milk Chicken with almonds

Preparation Time: 30 minute | Cook time: 20 minute | Servings 4

1 Tablespoon extra-virgin olive oil

1 small yellow onion, diced

2 garlic cloves, grated or minced

¼ Teaspoon salt

¼ Teaspoon freshly ground black pepper

½ Teaspoon curry powder, or more, to taste

½ cup red lentils, rinsed

3 medium carrots, sliced into 1-inch pieces

1½ cups chicken or Veggie Trimmings Stock, or water

1 Can full-fat coconut milk

Crushed almonds, for garnish

1. In a medium saucepan, heat the oil over medium heat.
2. Add the onion and cook until soft and translucent, about 2 minutes.
3. Add the garlic, salt, pepper, and curry powder and cook until fragrant, 30 to 60 seconds.
4. Add the lentils and carrots and pour in the stock and coconut milk. Bring to a boil, reduce the heat, and simmer until the carrots and lentils are soft, about 20 minutes.
5. Serve as it is or purée in a blender or food processor for a creamier consistency, if desired. Garnish with almonds.

Nutrition Facts

Calorie 372 | Fats 28g| Carbs 27g| Protein 9g

Spinach and Berry with Chicken Salad

Preparation Time: 15 minute | Cook time: 10 minute | Servings 4

4 small beets, peeled and chopped

1 tablespoon plus 1/4 cup olive oil, divided

1 pound boneless, skinless chicken breast

13/4 teaspoons salt, divided

3/4 teaspoon ground black pepper, divided

5 cups baby spinach

1 cup sliced strawberries

1/2 cup chopped pecans

2 tablespoons apple cider vinegar

2 tablespoons maple syrup

2 tablespoons orange juice

1. Place beets in a medium saucepan and cover with water. Boil beets in water until soft, about 20 minutes.

2. Drain beets and allow to cool completely.

3. Meanwhile, heat 1 tablespoon olive oil in a large nonstick frying pan over medium heat.

4. Season both sides of chicken with 3/4 teaspoon salt and 1/4 teaspoon pepper. Add chicken to the pan.

5. Cover the pan and cook until just cooked through, 5–8 minutes on each side. Transfer chicken to a cutting board and let cool.

6. Cut the chicken into bite-sized pieces.

7. In a large bowl, combine chicken, spinach, strawberries, pecans, and cooled beets.

8. In a separate small bowl, whisk together remaining olive oil, vinegar, maple syrup, and orange juice, and pour over salad, tossing well to coat.

9. Season with remaining salt and black pepper.

Nutrition Facts

Calorie 526| Fats 32g| Carbs 22g| Protein 39g

Best ever Coconut Chicken Soup with Mushrooms

Preparation Time: 30 minutes | Cook time: 20 minutes | Servings 6

1 Tablespoon olive oil

1 medium yellow onion, chopped

227 g sliced mushrooms, any variety

Salt and pepper to taste

2 tablespoons fresh minced garlic

1 Teaspoon fresh chopped thyme

1 cup canned coconut milk, whisked

1 cup chicken or vegetable broth

1. Heat the oil in a large saucepan over medium heat.

2. Stir in the onions and mushrooms then season with salt and pepper to taste.

3. Cook for 10 to 12 minutes until the mushroom liquid has cooked off.

4. Stir in the garlic and thyme then whisk in the coconut milk and chicken broth.

5. Bring to a simmer and cook on low heat for 8 to 10 minutes until thick.

6. Remove from heat and puree the soup with an immersion blender – serve hot.

Nutrition Facts

Calorie 200| Fats 15g| Carbs 7.5g| Protein 11g

Chilled Coconut Chicken Avocado Soup

Preparation Time: 30 minutes | Cook time: 0 minutes | Servings 4

4 ripe avocadoes, pitted and chopped

3 1/2 cups vegetable broth

2/3 cup canned coconut milk

3 small shallots, diced

3 Tablespoons dry white wine

Salt and pepper to taste

1. Combine the avocado, chicken broth and coconut milk in a blender. Blend until smooth and well combined.

2. Add the shallots, wine and salt and pepper – blend smooth.

3. Pour the mixture into a bowl then cover and chill at least 6 hours.

4. Spoon the soup into bowls and garnish with diced avocado and a pinch of cayenne to serve.

Nutrition Facts

Calorie 365| Fats 33g| Carbs 14g| Protein 6g

Super smooth Pumpkin & Ginger Chicken Soup

Preparation Time: 10 minutes | **Cook time:** 45 minutes | **Servings 5**

250 ml coconut milk

60 grams fresh ginger (about 3-4 thumb sized pieces)

1 Teaspoon ground cumin

1 Kilogram pumpkin

500 ml chicken broth or stock

250 ml coconut milk

1/2 Teaspoon ground cinnamon

2 tablespoons coconut oil for roasting the pumpkin

Salt and pepper to taste

1. Preheat oven to 180 C and line a large tray with baking paper.

2. Peel pumpkin and cut into even-sized chunks.

3. Place on tray, drizzle over olive oil and toss around with your hands to coat.

4. Roast pumpkin in the oven for approximately 45 minutes or until super soft and starting to caramelize at the edges.

5. Peel the ginger and gather the rest of the ingredients while the pumpkin is roasting.

6. Place cooked pumpkin, chicken broth/stock, coconut milk, ginger, cumin and cinnamon into blender jug.

7. Blend until super smooth. Season it with salt and pepper to taste.

8. Heat a portion of the soup in a saucepan over the stove, to serve (or microwave the soup if that's more convenient for you). Enjoy!

Nutrition Facts

Calorie 372| Fats 28g| Carbs27 g| Protein9 g

Paleo Lean Beef Vegetables Soup

Preparation Time: 15 minute | Cook time: 20 minute | Servings 14

1 pound 85% lean ground beef

1 small head cabbage, cored and chopped

2 green onions, chopped

1 medium red bell pepper, seeded and chopped

1 medium bunch celery, chopped

1 cup chopped carrots

4 cups Basic Vegetable Stock (see recipe in this chapter)

4 cups water

3 cloves garlic, peeled and minced

1/4 teaspoon crushed red pepper flakes

1/4 teaspoon dried basil

1/4 teaspoon dried oregano

1/4 teaspoon dried thyme

1/4 teaspoon onion powder

1. Heat a large skillet over medium-high heat. Add beef and cook, breaking up the lumps, until the meat is cooked through and just beginning to brown, 8–10 minutes. Drain excess fat.

2. Place beef, cabbage, green onions, bell pepper, celery, and carrots in a 6-quart slow cooker.

3. Pour in stock and water.

4. Stir in garlic, pepper flakes, basil, oregano, thyme, and onion powder. Cover and cook on low for 8–10 minutes.

Nutrition Facts

Calorie 107| Fats 5g| Carbs 8g| Protein 8g

Honey Garlic Paprika Salmon

Preparation Time: 10 minute | Cook time: 10 minute | Servings 4

3 Tablespoon butter

2 tsp olive oil

6 cloves garlic minced

1/2 cup honey

3 Tablespoon water

3 Tablespoon soy sauce

1 Tablespoon sriracha sauce

2 Tablespoon lemon juice4 (6 oz each) salmon filets

1/2 tsp kosher salt

1/2 tsp black pepper

1/2 tsp smoked paprika (or regular paprika)

1/4 tsp blackening seasoning (optional)

1. Pat salmon dry, then season with salt, pepper, paprika and blackening seasoning (if using). Set aside. Adjust oven rack to middle position, then preheat broiler.

2. Add butter and oil to a large, oven-safe skillet over high heat. Once hi is melted, add garlic, water, soy sauce, sriracha, honey and lemon juice and cook 30 seconds or so, until sauce is heated through.

3. Add salmon, skin side down (if using salmon with skin), and cook 3 minutes. While salmon cooks, baste frequently with sauce from the pan by spooning it over the top of the salmon.

4. Broil salmon for 5-6 minutes, basting with sauce once during the broil, until salmon is caramelized and cooked to desired doneness.

5. Garnish with minced parsley if desired.

Homemade Shrimp and Onions with Grits

Preparation Time: 10 minute | Cook time: 25 minute | Servings 4

1 lb. medium shrimp

1/8 onion, diced

1/2 cup butter

1 tablespoon garlic salt (or 1 garlic clove finely chopped)

1 tablespoon salt

1/2 tablespoon pepper

1/2 bell pepper (green)

1. Shell, clean and devein shrimp. Remove tails. Sprinkle with seasonings.

2. Melt butter in large skillet.

3. Add shrimp, bell pepper and onion and garlic if using. Cook over medium heat for 3-5 minutes.

4. Move skillet from side to side to keep onions moving and to discourage sticking. Watch closely. Do not overcook nor scorch onions.

5. Serve over white rice or grits.

Mushroom & Shrimp with Snow Peas

Preparation Time: 10 minute | Cook time: 20 minute | Servings 4

2 tablespoons corn-starch

1 teaspoon sugar

1 teaspoon chicken bouillon granules

1 teaspoon dill weed

1/2 teaspoon salt

1/2 teaspoon grated lemon zest

1/8 teaspoon pepper

1 cup water

3 tablespoons lemon juice

1 pound uncooked medium shrimp, peeled and deveined

2 cups sliced fresh mushrooms

1-1/2 cups sliced celery

1 medium sweet yellow or red pepper, julienned

1/4 cup thinly sliced green onions

1 tablespoon olive oil

6 ounces fresh or frozen snow peas, thawed

2 cups cooked rice

1. In a small bowl, combine the corn starch, sugar, bouillon, dill, salt, lemon zest and pepper. Stir in water and lemon juice until blended; set aside.

2. In a large nonstick skillet or wok, stir-fry the shrimp, mushrooms, celery, yellow pepper and onions in oil for 5 minutes.

3. Add the peas; stir-fry 1-2 minutes longer or until crisp-tender. Stir bouillon mixture; add to skillet.

4. Bring to a boil; cook and stir for 2 minutes or until thickened. Serve with rice.

Flounder Fillets with Celery Shrimp Stuffing

Preparation Time: 15 minute | Cook time: 20 minute | Servings 6

For Stuffing

6 tablespoons butter, cubed

1 small onion, finely chopped

1/4 cup finely chopped celery

1/4 cup finely chopped green pepper

1 pound uncooked shrimp, peeled, deveined and chopped

1/4 cup beef broth

1 teaspoon diced pimientos, drained

1 teaspoon Worcestershire sauce

1/2 teaspoon dill weeds

For Fish

6 flounder fillets (3 ounces each)

5 tablespoons butter, melted

2 tablespoons lemon juice

1 teaspoon minced fresh parsley

1/2 teaspoon paprika

Salt and pepper to taste

1. Preheat oven to 375°. In a large skillet, melt butter. Add onion, celery and green pepper; sauté until tender.

2. Add shrimp; cook and stir until shrimp turn pink.

3. Add broth, pimientos, Worcestershire sauce, dill, chives, salt and cayenne; heat through. Remove from heat; stir in bread crumbs. Spoon about 1/2 cup stuffing onto each fillet; roll up.

4. Place seam side down in a greased 13x9-in. baking dish. Drizzle with butter and lemon juice.

5. Sprinkle with seasonings. Bake, uncovered, 20-25 minutes or until fish flakes easily with a fork.

Shrimp Lettuce Garden Salad

Preparation Time: 15 minute | Cook time: 15 minute | Servings 6

1 head romaine lettuce- rinsed, dried and chopped

2 bunches radishes, sliced

1 bunch green onions, chopped

1 cucumber, cleaned and chopped

3 tomatoes, chopped

3 stalks celery, chopped

1 (4.5 ounce) can small shrimp, drained

1. In a large bowl, combine the Romaine, radishes, green onions, cucumber, tomatoes, celery and shrimp.

2. Toss with favourite salad dressing and serve.

Low Fat Buttery Oyster Stew

Preparation Time: 15 minute | Cook time: 30 minute | Servings 6

3 tablespoons butter

2 cups diced white onion

1 cup diced celery, plus 1/4 cup chopped celery leaves, divided

2 pints shucked oysters, liquid reserved

¾ teaspoon kosher salt

½ teaspoon paprika

3 ½ cups low-fat milk

½ cup heavy cream

3 dashes hot sauce

Freshly ground pepper to taste

2 tablespoons snipped fresh chives

1. Heat butter in a large saucepan over medium heat until melted. Add onion and diced celery; reduce heat to medium-low and cook, stirring occasionally, until translucent and very tender but not browned, 25 to 30 minutes.

2. Meanwhile, cut oysters in half or quarters, depending on size. Pour the oyster liquid through a fine-mesh sieve to strain out any grit.

3. Stir salt and paprika into the vegetables and cook, stirring, for 1 minute more. Add the strained oyster liquid, milk, cream and hot sauce. Increase heat to high and bring to a boil

4. Reduce heat to a simmer and gently add the oysters. Cook just until their edges begin to curl, 2 to 3 minute.

5. Remove from heat. Season with pepper. Garnish with celery leaves and chives.

EASY PEASY RECIPES

Quick Ginger-Garlic Miso Dressing

Preparation Time: 5 minute | Cook time: 30 minute | Makes 1 ¾ cups

1 cup Cauliflower Purée

⅔ cup brown rice vinegar

¼ cup mellow white miso

4 large cloves garlic, peeled

2 tablespoons minced fresh ginger

2 tablespoons brown rice syrup

½ teaspoon cayenne pepper

1. Combine all ingredients in a food processor and purée until smooth and creamy.

2. Store refrigerated in an airtight container for up to seven days.

Super Tasty and Creamy Shallot Mushrooms

Preparation Time: 5 minute | Cook time: 30 minute | Servings 8

1 cup hot water

2 shallots, minced

8 ounces cremini mushrooms (about 3-3½ cups), sliced

4 tablespoons arrowroot powder whisked together with ¼ cup cold water

2½ cups vegetable stock or Basic Soup Stock

6 tablespoons dry sherry

Sea salt and black pepper to taste

1. Place the dried porcini mushrooms in a medium bowl and pour the hot water over them. Let stand for about 20 minutes.

2. Strain the mushrooms and reserve the liquid. Coarsely chop the mushrooms.

3. Sauté the shallots, porcini mushrooms, and cremini mushrooms over medium-high heat for 7 to 8 minutes.

4. Add water 1 to 2 tablespoons at a time as needed to keep the vegetables from sticking.

5. Add the arrowroot mixture, vegetable stock, ½ cup of the reserved porcini mushroom soaking liquid, and sherry, and bring the gravy to a boil.

6. Cook until thickened and remove from the heat. Season with salt and pepper.

7. Serve hot.

Hot and Spicy Onion Ground Cumin Sauce

Preparation Time: 5 minute | Cook time: 15 minute | Makes 3 cups

1 small yellow onion, minced

2 cloves garlic, minced

1½ tablespoons ancho chili powder

2 teaspoons ground cumin

½ teaspoon oregano

3 cups Cauliflower Purée

Sea salt and black pepper to taste

1. Sauté the onion over medium heat for 10 minutes.

2. Add water 1 to 2 tablespoons at a time to keep the onion from sticking.

3. Add the garlic, chili powder, cumin, and oregano, and cook for another minute.

4. Add the cauliflower purée and cook for 2 to 4 minutes until the sauce is hot. Season with salt and pepper.

Protein rich Garlic Edamame Dip

Preparation Time: 10 minute | Cook time: 0 minute | Makes 3 cups

1 pound frozen shelled edamame, thawed

⅓ Cup tahini

2 tablespoons grated fresh ginger

3 teaspoons minced garlic (about 3 cloves)

2 tablespoons lemon juice (about 1 small lemon)

1 teaspoon salt

1 tablespoon sesame oil (optional)

1. In a food processor or high-speed blender, purée the edamame, tahini, ginger, garlic, lemon juice, and salt until smooth.

2. With the motor running, slowly drizzle in the sesame oil (if using) until creamy.

3. Transfer to a storage container and seal the lid.

Spicy Vegan Paprika Garlic Cashew Cream

Preparation Time: 5 minute | Cook time: 0 minute | Makes 1 ½ Cups

1 cup raw cashews

2½ cups water, divided

2 tablespoons lemon juice (about 1 small lemon)

½ teaspoon salt

½ teaspoon unseasoned rice vinegar or apple cider vinegar

2 teaspoons minced garlic (about 2 cloves)

1 teaspoon smoked paprika (optional)

1 tablespoon extra-virgin olive oil

1. In a small bowl, soak the raw cashews in 2 cups of water for 1 hour. Rinse and drain.

2. Transfer the cashews to a blender, and add the lemon juice, salt, vinegar, garlic, and paprika.

3. Blend at high speed, and slowly drizzle the olive oil into the mixture. If needed, slowly drizzle in the remaining ½ cup of water until you reach a thick, creamy consistency.

4. Transfer the cream into a glass jar. Close the lid tightly.

Barley Miso Mushroom Sauce

Preparation Time: 15 minute | Cook time: 30 minute | Makes 1 Quarts

13⁄4 cups vegetable broth or water

4 tablespoons barley miso (red or traditional)

1 onion, chopped

2 cups sliced mushrooms (about 1⁄2 pound)

Dash freshly ground pepper

2 to 3 teaspoons dried sage (to taste)

2 teaspoons dried thyme

4 tablespoons arrowroot, dissolved in 1⁄4 cup water

1. Bring the broth or water to a boil. Spoon the miso into the boiling liquid and stir to dissolve.

2. Add the onion, mushrooms, sage, and thyme. Simmer for 15 to 20 minutes, stirring occasionally.

3. Add the dissolved arrowroot to the mixture.

4. Stir until thickened, about 5 minutes.

5. Add a dash of fresh pepper and more miso if a stronger gravy taste is desired

Creamy Leek Mushroom Sage Sauce

Preparation Time: 10 minute | Cook time: 25 minute | Makes 2 cups

1/4 pound mushrooms (8 large), sliced

1 leek, washed and sliced

2 cups water

1 tablespoon soy sauce

Freshly ground white pepper

2 tablespoons cornstarch

1 teaspoon parsley flakes

1/4 teaspoon dried oregano

1/4 teaspoon dried sage

1/8 teaspoon paprika

1. Sauté the mushrooms and leek in 1/2 cup of the water for 5 minutes.
2. Add an additional 1 cup of water and all the seasonings.
3. Cook over low heat for 15 minutes.
4. Mix the cornstarch in the remaining 1/2 cup cold water.

5. Slowly add to the sauce while stirring. Cook, stirring, until thickened and clear.

Rich Garlic Soy Sauce

Preparation Time: 10 minute | Cook time: 10 minute | Servings 2

6 to 8 cloves garlic, thinly sliced

1 onion, sliced

One 8.45-ounce package low-fat plain soy milk

1 heaping tablespoon corn starch

1 heaping tablespoon brewer's yeast Garlic powder to taste (optional)

1. Sauté the garlic and onion in a small amount of water for 3 to 5 minutes.

2. In another pot, mix the soy milk, corn starch, and yeast.

3. Add the garlic, onion, and any water remaining in the sauté pan.

4. Bring to a boil and cook, stirring constantly, until thickened

5. Serve

Authentic Green Chili Tomato Sauce

Preparation Time: 10 minute | Cook time: 30 minute | Makes 3 Quarts 2

3½ cups water

Four 16-ounce cans whole tomatoes, chopped

Three 15-ounce cans tomato sauce

Four 7-ounce cans chopped green chillies

2 tablespoons diced jalapeño pepper

6 cloves garlic (or 2 tablespoons garlic powder)

1. Place all of the ingredients in a large pot and cook for 30 minutes or as long as possible.
2. Add garlic powder to taste

Golden Carrot Orange Honey Sauce

Preparation Time: 10 minute | Cook time: 10 minute | Makes 1 ½ cups

3 tablespoons whole-wheat pastry flour

¼ teaspoon salt (optional)

½ cup honey

⅔ cup boiling water

⅓ cup brandy (or 1 teaspoon brandy extract)

¼ cup minced carrot

2 tablespoons fresh-squeezed orange juice

2 tablespoons fresh lemon juice

Dash ground nutmeg

1. In small saucepan, combine the flour and salt. Dissolve the honey in the boiling water and add the brandy. (If extract is used, add it last and use ⅓ cup more water.)

2. Add the hot liquid mixture slowly to the flour mixture. Cook over medium heat for 5 minutes, or until thick and clear, stirring constantly.

3. Add the carrot, orange and lemon juices, and the nutmeg.

4. Simmer for 5 minutes longer

Creamy Garlic Cilantro Butter Dip

Preparation Time: 5 minute | Cook time: 30 minute | Makes 1 ½ Cups

4 bunches fresh cilantro

3 cloves garlic, peeled

3 to 4 tablespoons fresh lemon juice

2 tablespoons honey

1 to 2 tablespoons natural peanut butter

1. Wash the cilantro well and remove any yellowed leaves and tough stems. Place in a food processor with the garlic.

2. Process until finely chopped. Combine the lemon juice, honey, and peanut butter in a bowl.

3. Combine the two mixtures and mix well.

Scallions and Oyster Mushroom Sauce

Preparation Time: 20 minute | Cook time: 15 minute | Servings 6

4 cups water

3 ounces dried shiitake or oyster mushrooms

1 medium onion, chopped

1 bunch scallions, chopped

2 cloves garlic, minced

1½ tablespoons grated fresh ginger

1/3 cup soy sauce

1/4 cup sherry or rice vinegar

1/3 cup corn starch, mixed with 1/2 cup cold water

1. Boil 2 cups of the water and pour over the dried mushrooms in a bowl.

2. Soak for 15 minutes while you are chopping the vegetables.

3. Remove the mushrooms from the water and squeeze to remove excess water.

4. Strain the water and reserve 1 cup. Set aside.

5. Cut the tough stems off the mushrooms and discard.

6. Chop the mushrooms into bite-sized pieces. Set aside.

7. Put the 1 cup of reserved mushroom liquid into a saucepan. Add the chopped onion. Cook, stirring occasionally, until the onion softens, 2 to 3 minutes.

8. Add the scallions, garlic, ginger, soy sauce, sherry or rice vinegar, and the chopped mushrooms.

9. Mix well and add the remaining 2 cups of water. Heat to boiling, stirring occasionally.

10. Add the corn starch mixture and cook, stirring continually, until thickened and clear.

Classic Pepper Sauce

Preparation Time: 10 minute | Cook time: 20 minute | Makes 1 cup

2 large red bell peppers, chopped

1 small onion, chopped

2 cloves garlic, minced

1⁄8 teaspoon white pepper

1⁄4 cup water

11⁄2 teaspoons white-wine vinegar

1⁄8 teaspoon crushed red pepper flakes

Dash or two Tabasco

1⁄2 to 1 tablespoon horseradish (optional)

1. Place the bell peppers, onion, and garlic in a saucepan with the water.
2. Cover and cook over low heat until the peppers are very soft, about 15 minutes.
3. Transfer to a food processor or blender and process until smooth. Return to the saucepan.
4. Add the remaining ingredients.
5. Cook over low heat for 5 minutes, stirring occasionally, to allow the flavors to blend

Hot and Spicy Yellow Pepper-Potato Puree

Preparation Time: 15 minute | Cook time: 30 minute | Servings 6

4 medium yellow bell peppers

2 medium potatoes

1 cup water

2 tablespoons white wine

1 tablespoon fresh lemon juice

1½ teaspoons soy sauce

1 teaspoon onion powder

¼ teaspoon freshly ground white pepper

1. Clean and chop the peppers and peel and chop the potatoes. Place in a saucepan with the water.

2. Cover and cook over low heat for 30 minutes.

3. Remove from the heat. Pour into a blender or food processor. Blend until smooth.

4. Return to the saucepan and add the remaining ingredients.

5. Heat through to allow the flavors to blend.

Super Simple Marinara Bell Pepper Sauce

Preparation Time: 20 minute | Cook time: 30 minute | Servings 6

1 cup diced green bell pepper

1 cup diced onion

1 cup shredded carrot

1 cup shredded celery

1 cup sliced mushrooms

3 cloves garlic, minced

1 cup water

15- to 16-ounce can whole tomatoes, chopped, with liquid

One 28-ounce can crushed tomatoes or tomato puree

1/4 cup nonalcoholic red wine

1 tablespoon parsley flakes

1 small bay leaf

3/4 teaspoon dried basil

3/4 teaspoon dried oregano

1/2 teaspoon dried thyme

1/4 teaspoon dried tarragon

1. Place the vegetables and garlic in a large pot with the water. Cook, stirring, until slightly tender, about 10 minutes.

2. Add the remaining ingredients and cook, uncovered, for 35 minutes. Remove the bay leaf before serving.

Fresh Zucchini Thyme Sauce

Preparation Time: 10 minute | Cook time: 25 minute | Servings 4

½ medium onion, chopped 2 cloves garlic, pressed

1 to 2 zucchini, chunked ½ cup water

Three 8-ounce cans tomato sauce

1 teaspoon dried basil

1 teaspoon dried thyme

1 teaspoon dried oregano

2 to 4 drops Tabasco or ½ teaspoon crushed red pepper flakes

1. Sauté the onion, garlic, and zucchini in the water for about 5 minutes.

2. Add the remaining ingredients and cook, uncovered, over low heat for 15 to 20 minutes.

Very Spicy Carrot and Butternut Squash Curry

Preparation Time: 20 minutes | Cook time: 30 minutes | Servings 4

1 cup dry chickpeas (garbanzo beans)

2 tablespoons vegetable oil

2 onions, chopped

4 cloves garlic, minced

6 pods green cardamom

2 dried red Chile peppers, stemmed and seeded

2 teaspoons coriander seeds

2 teaspoons ground turmeric

1 teaspoon black mustard seeds

1 tablespoon tomato paste, or more to taste

1 large butternut squash, peeled and cut into 1-inch cubes

3 carrots, chopped

1 ½ cups water, or as needed

½ bunch fresh cilantro, chopped

1. Place chickpeas in a large bowl and cover with cold water. Let soak, 8 hours to overnight.

2. Drain and rinse chickpeas under running cold water.

3. Place in a large pot, cover with several inches of water, and bring to a boil.

4. Reduce heat and simmer until chickpeas are soft, 20 to 25 minutes. Drain.

5. When chickpeas are halfway done, heat oil in a large pot and cook onions until soft and translucent, about 5 minutes.

6. Stir in garlic and cook until fragrant, about 30 seconds.

7. Add cardamom pods, Chile peppers, coriander seeds, turmeric, and mustard seeds and toast for 1 minute. Mix in tomato paste

8. Stir butternut squash and carrots into the pot.

9. Add enough water to cover vegetables halfway. Simmer over low heat, partially covered, until all the vegetables are soft.

10. Mix in cooked chickpeas shortly before serving and heat until warm. Serve sprinkled with cilantro.

Five Spiced Almonds Celery Fry

Preparation Time: 15 minute | Cook time: 10 minute | Servings 4

2 tablespoons olive oil

2 cloves garlic, peeled and minced

3 cups sliced celery

1/4 cup water

1 tablespoon coconut amino

1/2 teaspoon five-spice powder

1/2 cup chopped celery leaves

1/8 teaspoon crushed red pepper flakes

1/3 cup sliced almonds, toasted

1. In a large saucepan, heat olive oil over medium heat.

2. Add garlic; cook for 1 minute.

3. Add celery; cook for 2–3 minutes or until crisp-tender.

4. Add water and coconut amino; bring to a simmer.

5. Cover pan, reduce heat, and simmer for 4 minutes.

6. Uncover pan and add five-spice powder, celery leaves, and crushed red pepper flakes; cook for 2 minutes longer.

7. Sprinkle with almonds and serve immediately.

Crispy Onion and Tender Apple Mix

Preparation Time: 15 minute | Cook time: 15 minute | Servings 4

1 tablespoon grass-fed butter

1 tablespoon olive oil

2 medium onions, peeled and chopped

2 cloves garlic, peeled and minced

3 medium apples, peeled, cored, and sliced

3 tablespoons maple syrup

1 tablespoon lemon juice

1/2 teaspoon salt

1/2 teaspoon dried thyme leaves

1. In a large saucepan, melt butter and olive oil over medium heat.

2. Add onions and garlic and cook until crisp-tender, about 4 minutes.

3. Add apples and stir.

4. Drizzle with maple syrup and lemon juice, and sprinkle with salt and thyme leaves.

5. Cover and cook on low for about 7–9 minutes or until apples are tender. Serve immediately.

One Pan Mushroom with Sautéed Almonds

Preparation Time: 15 minute | Cook time: 10 minute | Servings 4

1 pound fresh green beans, trimmed and chopped

2 tablespoons olive oil

1/3 cup sliced almonds

3/4 cup sliced mushrooms

1/2 medium yellow onion, peeled and chopped

1/2 teaspoon lemon juice

1. Fill a medium saucepan with cold salted water and bring to a boil over high heat.

2. Add beans and cook until they are a vibrant green, about 3–4 minutes.

3. Drain and rinse under cold water.

4. Heat olive oil in a large skillet over medium heat.

5. Sauté almonds, mushrooms, and onion for 3–4 minutes, stirring frequently.

6. Add green beans and lemon juice and heat for another 2 minutes.

Spicy Onion Collard Greens Mix

Preparation Time: 15 minute | Cook time: 30 minute | Servings 4

2 tablespoons olive oil

1 medium onion, peeled and diced

3 cloves garlic, peeled and minced

1 pound collard greens, chopped

3/4 cup water

1 (14-ounce) can diced tomatoes, drained

11/2 teaspoons Cajun seasoning

1/2 teaspoon hot sauce

1/4 teaspoon salt

1. In a large skillet, heat olive oil over medium heat.

2. Add onion, garlic, and collard greens and sauté for 3–5 minutes until onions are soft.

3. Add water, tomatoes, and Cajun seasoning.

4. Bring to a simmer over low heat, cover, and allow to cook for 20 minutes, or until greens are soft, stirring occasionally.

5. Remove lid, stir in hot sauce and salt, and cook, uncovered, for another 1–2 minutes, to allow excess moisture to evaporate.

Three-Pepper Garlic Dish

Preparation Time: 15 minute | Cook time: 30 minute | Servings 4

1/4 cup olive oil

2 large green bell peppers

2 large yellow bell peppers

2 large red bell peppers

6 cloves garlic, peeled and minced

1 teaspoon ground black pepper

1. Preheat grill or broiler and Pour olive oil into a large bowl.

2. Dip peppers in olive oil, then place peppers on grill or a broiler pan. Reserve remaining oil.

3. Grill or broil peppers, turning frequently, until skin is blistered and beginning to blacken.

4. Place peppers in a paper bag and fold over the top of the bag.

5. Let peppers steam in the bag for 10 minutes.

6. Remove peppers from bag and peel off the blistered skin.

7. Slice peppers and return them to the bowl with olive oil, along with garlic and black pepper.

8. Serve at room temperature or store in the refrigerator for up to three days.

Spicy Peppery Green Beans with Baby Peas

Preparation Time: 15 minute | Cook time: 15 minute | Servings 4

1 pound fresh green beans, trimmed and chopped

1 tablespoon olive oil

1 tablespoon sesame oil

1 (10-ounce) package frozen baby peas, thawed

4 cloves garlic, peeled and minced

1 teaspoon minced fresh ginger

1/2 teaspoon crushed red pepper flakes

1 teaspoon salt

1/2 teaspoon ground black pepper

1. Fill a medium saucepan with cold salted water and bring to a boil over high heat.
2. Add beans and cook until they are a vibrant green, about 3–4 minutes.
3. Drain and rinse under cold water.
4. Heat olive oil and sesame oil in a large skillet.
5. Add green beans, peas, garlic, ginger, and red pepper flakes.
6. Cook, stirring frequently, for 10 minutes until garlic is soft.
7. Season with salt and black pepper.

Green Beans Dry Fry with Rosemary

Preparation Time: 15 minute | Cook time: 30 minute | Servings 4

1 pound green beans

1 tablespoon minced rosemary

1 teaspoon minced thyme

2 tablespoons lemon juice

2 tablespoons water

1. Place all ingredients in a cooker.

2. Stir to distribute spices evenly.

3. Cook for 30 minutes or until green beans are tender.

4. Stir before serving.

Lemony Garlic Broccoli with Hazelnuts

Preparation Time: 15 minute | Cook time: 30 minute | Servings 4

2 pounds broccoli florets, washed and trimmed

12 cloves garlic, peeled

1/2 teaspoon ground black pepper

1 cup large raw hazelnuts

2 tablespoons olive oil

Juice from 2 medium lemons

1. Place broccoli in a cooker and add garlic, pepper, hazelnuts, olive oil, and lemon juice and toss.

2. Cover and cook on high for 30 minutes

3. Serve and enjoy!

Green Beans Shallot Stir Fry

Preparation Time: 15 minute | Cook time: 30 minute | Servings 4

11/2 pounds fresh green beans, trimmed

3 tablespoons olive oil

3 large shallots, peeled and cut into thin wedges

6 cloves garlic, peeled and sliced

1 tablespoon grated lemon zest

1/2 teaspoon ground black pepper

1/2 cup water

1. Place green beans in a greased (with coconut oil) cooker.

2. Add remaining ingredients over the top of the beans.

3. Cook on high for 30 minutes.

4. Serve and enjoy!

Cashew and Peppery Asparagus fry

Preparation Time: 15 minute | Cook time: 15 minute | Servings 4

2 tablespoons olive oil

2 tablespoons sesame oil

1 teaspoon minced fresh gingerroot

1 pound asparagus ends trimmed and cut into 2" pieces

1 teaspoon crushed red pepper flakes

1/2 cup chopped cashews

1. Heat olive oil and sesame oil in a wok or large skillet over low heat.

2. Add ginger and stir-fry until slightly brown, about 5 minutes.

3. 2 Add asparagus and red pepper flakes, and stir-fry for 5 minutes.

4. Add cashews. Cook, stirring frequently, for about 5 minutes or until asparagus is tender.

Hot and Spicy Garlic Broccoli with Bell Peppers

Preparation Time: 15 minute | Cook time: 15 minute | Servings 4

1 medium head broccoli

2 tablespoons coconut oil

1 medium onion, peeled and chopped

1 medium red bell pepper, seeded and chopped

1 medium orange bell pepper, seeded and chopped

3 cloves garlic, peeled and sliced

3 tablespoons water

1/2 teaspoon salt

1/8 teaspoon ground black pepper

1. Cut the florets off the broccoli stems. Peel stems and cut into 1" slices.

2. In a medium saucepan, steam broccoli until crisp-tender, about 3–4 minutes. Drain and set aside.

3. In a large skillet, melt coconut oil over medium heat. Add onion and cook for 3 minutes.

4. Add bell peppers and cook for another 3 minutes, stirring occasionally. Add broccoli, garlic, water, salt, and black pepper to skillet.

5. Bring to a simmer, then cover and simmer for 3–4 minutes until everything is hot.

Roasted Apples Brussels Mix

Preparation Time: 15 minute | Cook time: 25 minute | Servings 4

2 cups quartered Brussels sprouts

8 cloves garlic, peeled

2 tablespoons olive oil

2 tablespoons apple cider vinegar

3/4 teaspoon salt

1/2 teaspoon ground black pepper

2 medium apples, peeled, cored, and chopped

1. Preheat oven to 425°F.

2. Arrange Brussels sprouts and garlic in a single layer on a large baking sheet.

3. Drizzle with olive oil and apple cider vinegar and season with salt and black pepper.

4. Roast for 10–12 minutes, tossing once.

5. Remove tray from oven and add apples, tossing gently to combine.

6. Roast for 10 more minutes or until apples are soft, tossing once again.

Steamed Buttery Squash

Preparation Time: 15 minute | Cook time: 30 minute | Servings 4

1/4 cup maple syrup

1 teaspoon ground cinnamon

1 teaspoon ground nutmeg

2 small acorn squash, halved and seeded

3/4 cup raisins

4 tablespoons grass-fed butter

1/2 cup water

1. In a small bowl, combine maple syrup, cinnamon, and nutmeg.

2. Spoon maple syrup mixture into the squash halves. Sprinkle with raisins.

3. Top each half with 1 tablespoon butter.

4. Wrap each squash half individually in aluminum foil and seal tightly. Pour water into a cooker.

5. Place wrapped squash, cut side up, in the slow cooker.

6. Cover and cook on high for 30 minutes or until squash is tender.

7. Open the foil packets carefully to allow steam to escape.

Easy Tasty Veggie mix

Preparation Time: 15 minute | Cook time: 30 minute | Servings 4

1 pound plum tomatoes, chopped

1 medium eggplant, cut into 1/2" pieces

2 medium zucchini, cut into 1/2" pieces

3 medium stalks celery, sliced

1 large onion, peeled and finely chopped

1/2 cup chopped fresh parsley

1 teaspoon lemon juice

2 tablespoons lime juice

1 tablespoon maple syrup

1/4 cup raisins

1/4 cup tomato paste

1/4 teaspoon ground black pepper

1. Combine all ingredients in a cooker.
2. Cover and cook on low for 30 minutes.

Asian Sesame Apple Salad

Preparation Time: 15 minute | Cook time: 0 minute | Servings 4

2 cups packaged coleslaw mix

1 large unpeeled tart apple, cored and chopped

1/2 cup chopped celery

1/2 cup chopped green pepper

1/4 cup flaxseed oil

2 tablespoons lemon juice

1 teaspoon sesame seeds

1. In a medium bowl combine coleslaw mix, apple, celery, and green pepper.

2. In a small bowl, whisk together remaining ingredients.

3. Pour over coleslaw and toss to coat.

Vanilla Coconut Tender Squash & Walnuts

Preparation Time: 15 minute | Cook time: 30 minute | Servings 4

1 (2-pound) butternut squash, peeled, seeded, and cut into 1" cubes

1/2 cup water

1/2 cup maple syrup

1 cup chopped walnuts

1 teaspoon cinnamon

4 tablespoons coconut butter

2 teaspoons grated fresh ginger

1 teaspoon vanilla

1. Grease a 4-quart slow cooker with olive oil.

2. Add squash and water to a cooker.

3. In a small bowl mix together maple syrup, walnuts, cinnamon, coconut butter, ginger, and vanilla.

4. Drizzle maple syrup mixture evenly over butternut squash.

5. Cook on high for 30 minutes, or until squash is fork tender.

Quinoa and Cinnamon Butternut Squash Salad

Preparation Time: 15 minute | Cook time: 20 minute | Servings 4

3 cups peeled, seeded, and cubed butternut squash

1 tablespoon ground cinnamon

1 teaspoon nutmeg

2 cups water

1 cup uncooked quinoa

1. Preheat oven to 350°F.

2. Place squash in 9" × 11" baking dish. Sprinkle with cinnamon and nutmeg. Bake for 15 minutes or until tender and slightly brown.

3. Meanwhile, fill a medium pot with water, add quinoa, and bring to a boil. When water boils, reduce heat to low and cover; simmer 10 minutes.

4. Remove from heat and keep covered an additional 5 minutes; then fluff with a fork and set aside.

Tender Tomato Asparagus with pepper

Preparation Time: 15 minute | Cook time: 30 minute | Servings 4

1 pound asparagus, trimmed

1 (28-ounce) can petite diced tomatoes

1/2 cup peeled, chopped onion

4 cloves garlic, peeled and minced

3/4 teaspoon dried oregano

3/4 teaspoon basil

1 teaspoon ground black pepper

1. Combine all ingredients except pepper in a smaller slow cooker and cover.

2. Cook on high for about 30 minutes or until asparagus is tender. Season with pepper.

Tender Orangey Butternut Squash

Preparation Time: 15 minute | Cook time: 30 minute | Servings 4

5 cups peeled, seeded, and cubed butternut squash

1/4 cup maple syrup

1 tablespoon orange zest

1/2 teaspoon ground cinnamon

1/2 teaspoon ground cloves

1. Add all ingredients to a greased (with coconut oil) cooker.

2. Cook on high for 30 minutes until squash is fork tender.

Low Sodium Turnip Salad

Preparation Time: 15 minute | Cook time: 30 minute | Servings 4

4 medium turnips, peeled and cubed

2 tablespoons olive oil

2 tablespoons maple syrup

1 tablespoon brown mustard

1/4 teaspoon ground black pepper

1. Place turnips in a cooker, drizzle with olive oil and toss.

2. In a small bowl, mix together remaining ingredients.

3. Drizzle over turnips and mix well.

4. Cover and cook on low for 30 minutes.

Roasted Carrot Parsnips & Sweet Potato Bowl

Preparation Time: 15 minute | Cook time: 30 minute | Servings 4

3 medium carrots, peeled and chopped

2 small parsnips, peeled and chopped

2 medium sweet potatoes, peeled and chopped

2 tablespoons olive oil

1 teaspoon salt

1/2 teaspoon ground black pepper

1/4 cup maple syrup

2 tablespoons Dijon mustard

1 tablespoon apple cider vinegar

1/2 teaspoon hot sauce

1. Preheat oven to 400°F.

2. On a large baking sheet, spread out carrots, parsnips, and sweet potatoes in a single layer.

3. Drizzle with olive oil and season with salt and black pepper. Roast for 40 minutes, tossing once.

4. In a small bowl, whisk together maple syrup, Dijon mustard, apple cider vinegar, and hot sauce.

5. Transfer roasted vegetables to a large bowl and toss well with maple mixture.

Maple based Walnut and Beets with Goat Cheese

Preparation Time: 15 minute | Cook time: 30 minute | Servings 4

11/2 pounds beets

2 cups hot water

1/4 cup peeled, finely chopped red onion

2 tablespoons maple syrup

2 cloves garlic, peeled and minced

4 tablespoons chopped toasted walnuts

3 tablespoons lemon juice

1 tablespoon coconut oil

1 ounce crumbled goat cheese

1 teaspoon ground black pepper

1. Combine beets and water in a 4–6-quart slow cooker. Cover and cook on high for about 15 minutes or until beets are tender.

2. Drain and peel beets and cut into 3/4" cubes. Combine cubed beets and remaining ingredients, except goat cheese and black pepper, in the cooker.

3. Cover and cook on high for 15 minutes.

4. Top with goat cheese and season with black pepper before serving.

Coconut Glazed Carrots

Preparation Time: 15 minute | Cook time: 30 minute | Servings 4

1 tablespoon coconut oil

2 tablespoons maple syrup

1 teaspoon coconut amino

1 pound carrots, peeled and chopped

1. Preheat oven to 400°F. In large ovenproof saucepan, combine coconut oil and maple syrup and heat on stovetop until melted.

2. Add coconut amino and carrots; cook and stir for 2 minutes.

3. Place the pan in the oven and roast for 15–20 minutes, turning once, or until carrots are tender and glazed. Serve immediately.

Vegan Carrots and Peas Bowl

Preparation Time: 15 minute | Cook time: 10 minute | Servings 4

1 cup water

2 tablespoons lemon juice

2 tablespoons lime juice

1 pound carrots, peeled and julienned

1 (10-ounce) package frozen baby peas, thawed

1 tablespoon extra-virgin olive oil

1. In a large saucepan over medium-high heat, combine water, lemon juice, lime juice, and carrots.

2. Cover and cook until carrots are tender, about 10 minutes. Remove from heat and cool.

3. In a medium bowl, combine carrots, peas and olive oil. Stir to coat.

Garlic roasted Rabe and Kale

Preparation Time: 15 minute | Cook time: 30 minute | Servings 4

1 pound broccoli rabe, trimmed and cut into 2" pieces

1 pound kale, trimmed and cut into 4" pieces

2 tablespoons olive oil

1 medium onion, peeled and chopped

3 cloves garlic, peeled and minced

2 tablespoons lemon juice

1 teaspoon salt

1/8 teaspoon ground white pepper

1. In a medium saucepan, steam broccoli rabe and kale for about 3 minutes. Drain and set aside.

2. In a large skillet, heat olive oil over medium heat.

3. Add onion and garlic; cook and stir until tender, about 5 minutes.

4. Add steamed broccoli rabe and kale to skillet; cook and stir for 3 minutes.

5. Add lemon juice, salt, and white pepper and cook for another 2–3 minutes until tender. Serve immediately.

Classic Root Vegetables Recipe

Preparation Time: 15 minute | Cook time: 30 minute | Servings 4

1 pound parsnips, peeled and diced

1 pound turnips, peeled and diced

2 medium onions, peeled and chopped

1 pound carrots, peeled and diced

6 dried apricots, chopped

4 pitted prunes, chopped

1 teaspoon ground turmeric

1 teaspoon ground cumin

1/2 teaspoon ground ginger

1/2 teaspoon ground cinnamon

1/4 teaspoon ground cayenne pepper

1 tablespoon dried parsley

1 tablespoon dried cilantro

14 ounces Basic Vegetable Stock

1. Add parsnips, turnips, onions, carrots, apricots, prunes, turmeric, cumin, ginger, cinnamon, cayenne pepper, parsley, and cilantro to a cooker.

2. Pour in stock. Cover and cook on low for 30 minutes or until vegetables are cooked.

Warm Chipotle Sweet Potatoes Mash

Preparation Time: 15 minute | Cook time: 30 minute | Servings 4

3 pounds sweet potatoes, peeled and cubed

11/2 tablespoons ghee

11/4 teaspoons chipotle powder

Juice from 1/2 large lime

1. In a large saucepan fitted with a steamer insert, heat 1" water over medium-high heat.

2. Place sweet potatoes in steamer and steam until soft, approximately 5–8 minutes. Transfer to a large bowl.

3. In a small saucepan, heat ghee and whisk in chipotle powder and lime juice.

4. Pour mixture over sweet potatoes and mash with fork or potato masher.

Orange & Tomato based Fennel

Preparation Time: 15 minute | Cook time: 30 minute | Servings 4

3 small fennel bulbs, halved

1 (13-ounce) can chopped tomatoes

Rind and juice from 1 small orange

2 tablespoons maple syrup

1/2 teaspoon ground black pepper

1. Place fennel in a 4–6-quart slow cooker.

2. In a large mixing bowl, combine remaining ingredients.

3. Pour mixture over fennel.

4. Cover and cook on high for 30 minutes.

Fresh Vegan Coconut Jicama with White Pepper

Preparation Time: 15 minute | Cook time: 15 minute | Servings 4

1 large jicama

1 tablespoon lemon juice

2 tablespoons coconut oil

2 shallots, minced

1/2 teaspoon salt

1/8 teaspoon ground white pepper

1. Peel jicama and grate on a box grater or in the food processor.

2. Sprinkle with lemon juice and mix.

3. In a large skillet, melt coconut oil over medium heat.

4. Add shallots; cook and stir until tender, about 4 minutes.

5. Add grated jicama to the skillet; cook and stir until jicama releases some of its water and the water evaporates, about 5–6 minutes.

6. Taste jicama to see if it's tender.

7. If not, cook another 1–2 minutes. Then sprinkle with salt and white pepper and serve.

Garlicky Coconut Cabbage Curry

Preparation Time: 15 minute | Cook time: 15 minute | Servings 4

3 tablespoons coconut oil

1 medium onion, peeled and chopped

3 cloves garlic, peeled and minced

4 cups chopped green cabbage

3 cups chopped red cabbage

1/4 cup water

1 tablespoon coconut amino

1 teaspoon salt

1/8 teaspoon ground black pepper

1. In a large skillet, heat coconut oil over medium heat.

2. Add onion and garlic; cook and stir until crisp-tender, about 4 minutes.

3. Add cabbages to the skillet and cook and stir for 4 minutes.

4. Add water, coconut amino, salt, and black pepper and bring to a simmer.

5. Cover and cook for 5–7 minutes longer until cabbage is tender.

Three ingredients Vegetables Fruit Salad

Preparation Time: 15 minute | Cook time: 30 minute | Servings 4

1 large head red cabbage, sliced

2 medium onions, peeled and chopped

6 small tart apples, peeled, cored, and quartered

1 cup hot water

1 cup apple juice

2 tablespoons maple syrup

2/3 cup lime juice

1/2 teaspoon caraway seeds

3 tablespoons grass-fed butter, melted

3 tablespoons olive oil

1. Place cabbage, onions, and apples in a cooker that has been greased with coconut oil.

2. In a medium bowl whisk together water, apple juice, maple syrup, lime juice, and caraway seeds. Pour over cabbage.

3. Drizzle butter and olive oil over everything and cover cooker. Cook on high for 30 minutes. Stir well before serving.

Simple and Easy Tender Lemony Artichokes

Preparation Time: 15 minute | Cook time: 30 minute | Servings 4

3 large artichokes

1 cup water

1 large lemon, cut into eighths

2 tablespoons lemon juice

1 teaspoon dried oregano

1. Place artichokes stem side down in a cooker.
2. Pour water into the bottom of the slow cooker.
3. Add lemon slices, lemon juice, and oregano.
4. Cook on high for 30 minutes or until leaves are tender.

Lemony Shredded Cabbage Salad

Preparation Time: 15 minute | Cook time: 0 minute | Servings 4

1 teaspoon celery seed

11/2 cups lime juice

11/2 teaspoons mustard seed

1 teaspoon turmeric

1 teaspoon lemon juice

8 cups shredded cabbage

2 medium green bell peppers, seeded and finely chopped

1 large onion, peeled and finely chopped

1. In a small saucepan over high heat, bring celery seed, lime juice, mustard seed, turmeric, and lemon juice to a boil.

2. Place cabbage, bell peppers, and onion in a 2-quart or smaller baking dish with a cover.

3. Pour boiling liquid over vegetables. Cover and let stand for 2 hours. Serve at room temperature or chilled. This salad will keep crisp for three to four weeks in the refrigerator.

One pan Roasted vegetables with jalapeño peppers

Preparation Time: 15 minute | Cook time: 30 minute | Servings 4

1/4 cup olive oil

3 tablespoons apple cider vinegar

1 tablespoon minced garlic

1 pound asparagus stem ends trimmed

1 pound mixed summer squashes, thinly sliced

1 pound mini sweet peppers, stemmed and sliced in half lengthwise

2 medium jalapeño peppers, seeded and chopped

1 teaspoon seasoning salt

1. Preheat oven to 400°F.

2. In a small bowl, mix together olive oil, vinegar, and garlic and set aside.

3. Place all vegetables in a large roasting pan and toss.

4. Pour olive oil mixture over top, lifting and gently mixing the vegetables so they are all coated with oil. Sprinkle with seasoning salt.

5. Roast uncovered for about 25 minutes or until vegetables begin to darken; stir occasionally. Serve hot.

Almond Strawberry Pumpkin Salad

Preparation Time: 15 minutes | Cook time: 10 minutes | Servings 16

1 cup raw almonds

1 cup pumpkin seeds

1/2 cup sunflower seeds

1 cup dehydrated strawberries

1/2 cup goji berries

1. Combine all ingredients in a medium bowl.
2. Serve immediately or store in an airtight container at room temperature for up to one week.

Nutrition Facts

Calorie 139 | Fats 10g | Carbs 7g | Protein 5g

Mulberry-Pistachio Salad

Preparation Time: 15 minutes | Cook time: 10 minutes | Servings 12

1/2 cup pistachio nuts

1/2 cup pumpkin seeds

1/2 cup sunflower seeds

1/2 cup unsweetened coconut flakes

1 cup dried mulberries

1. Combine all ingredients in a medium bowl. S
2. Serve immediately or store in an airtight container at room temperature for up to one week.

Nutrition Facts

Calorie 140 | Fats 10g | Carbs 10g | Protein 5g

Tasty Cashew Pepper Cheese dip

Preparation Time: 5 minutes | Cook time: 0 minutes | Servings 2

1 cup raw cashews

2 teaspoons lemon juice

¼ teaspoon salt

¼ teaspoons freshly ground black pepper

3 tablespoons cold water, plus more as needed

1. Soak the cashews in a bowl of water to cover for at least 1 hour and up to overnight in the refrigerator.

2. Drain, briefly rinse, and transfer the cashews to a food processor.

3. Add the lemon juice, salt, and pepper and pulse until combined, about 1 minute.

4. Scrape down the sides of the food processor with a rubber spatula, add the water, and process until smooth, 2 to 4 minutes, adding more water by the teaspoon to thin it out if needed.

5. Add optional dip flavors and process until combined.

6. Serve with Gluten-Free Seedy Crackers.

Nutrition Facts

Calorie 351 | Fats 26g | Carbs 17g | Protein 11g

Homemade-Coconut Oil Baked Seeds Mix

Preparation Time: 10 minutes | **Cook time:** 30 minutes | **Servings 6**

¾ cup sesame seeds

⅓ cup sunflower seeds

¼ cup chia seeds

3 tablespoons pepitas (pumpkin seeds)

2 tablespoons flaxseeds

1 ⅔ cups water

1 teaspoon salt

3 tablespoons coconut oil, melted

1. Preheat the oven to 350°F.

2. In a large bowl, combine the seeds with the water and let them soak until they have absorbed the liquid and a thick dough forms, about 20 minutes.

3. Add the salt and stir well to combine.

4. Lightly grease a baking sheet with 1 tablespoon of the melted coconut oil.

5. Using a rubber spatula or wooden spoon, spread the dough in a thin layer (¼ inch or less) on the baking sheet.

6. Brush the top with the remaining 2 tablespoons coconut oil and bake until set and slightly browned on one side.

7. Remove the baking sheet from the oven.

8. Cool enough to handle, carefully break the cracker into smaller pieces.

Nutrition Facts

Calorie 262 | Fats 23g | Carbs 10g | Protein 7g

Salty Brown Apple

Preparation Time: 7 minutes | Cook time: 30 minutes | Servings 4

2 apples, cored

¼ teaspoon salt

1. Preheat the oven to 275°F. Line a baking sheet with aluminium foil or parchment paper.

2. Using a mandolin or sharp knife, thinly slice the apples. Spread them out flat on the prepared baking sheet in an even layer.

3. Sprinkle evenly with the salt and, if desired, other spices

4. Bake until crisp on one side, about 20 minutes, Turn the slices over and bake until completely crisped and lightly browned.

5. Remove from the oven and allow cooling before storing.

Nutrition Facts

Calorie 58 | Fats 0g | Carbs 15g | Protein 0g

Chilled Coconut Banana Dessert

Preparation Time: 4 minutes | Cook time: 0 minutes | Servings 4

4 bananas, peeled and sliced into 2-inch pieces

¼ cup unsweetened flaked coconut

¼ cup coconut milk

2 tablespoons almond butter

1. Freeze the bananas for at least an hour or overnight.
2. Add the bananas to a food processor or blender. Pulse a few times to break down.
3. Add the flaked coconut, coconut milk, and almond butter and process until smooth, 3 to 4 minutes.
4. Scrape down the sides of the food processor and serve immediately in chilled bowls or freeze for later enjoyment.

Nutrition Facts

Calorie 412 | Fats 20g | Carbs 60g | Protein 7g

Macadamia Snack with Egg fills and Raspberry Sauce

Preparation Time: 10 minutes | Cook time: 20 minutes | Makes 12 triangles

For Crust

3 cups raw macadamia nuts

½ cup coconut oil, melted

¼ teaspoon ground cinnamon

For filling

4 large eggs, at room temperature

3 tablespoons grated lemon zest (from 3 to 4 lemons)

½ cup lemon juice (from about 4 lemons)

½ cup coconut oil

2 tablespoons maple syrup

1 teaspoon alcohol-free vanilla extract

For sauce

1 cup fresh raspberries

1 teaspoon water

1. Preheat the oven to 350°F.

2. To make the crust, into a food processor put the nuts, coconut oil, and cinnamon and pulse until slightly chunky but sticky and dough-like.

3. Into the bottom of a 9-inch round tart pan, pie plate, or spring form pan, press the crust mixture.

4. Bake until the crust is set and slightly golden, about 10 minutes. Remove it from the oven and let it cool.

5. To make the filling, in a medium bowl beat the eggs; set aside.

6. Into a small saucepan put the lemon zest and juice, coconut oil, maple syrup, and vanilla and whisk to combine. Heat over medium heat until warm.

7. Spoon a few tablespoons of the heated mixture into the eggs, whisking constantly to temper the eggs.

8. Add the egg mixture to the saucepan, reduce the heat to medium-low, and cook until thickened, whisking constantly.

9. Pour the lemon filling into the crust, spreading it with a rubber spatula or wooden spoon into an even layer.

10. Refrigerate until firmly set (it shouldn't jiggle when you shake it), about 1 hour.

11. Meanwhile, make the sauce. In a saucepan, heat the raspberries and water over medium heat, whisking until smooth with some chunks.

12. Heat until warmed through and slightly thickened.

13. To serve, cut the tart into quarters and then cut each quarter into three small triangles.

14. Top with the raspberry sauce.

Nutrition Facts

Calorie 190 | Fats 12g | Carbs 49g | Protein 2g

Vanilla flavored Berry Mix Bowl

Preparation Time: 5 minutes | Cook time: 0 minutes | Servings 2

1 (14-ounce) can full-fat coconut milk, chilled

½ teaspoon alcohol-free vanilla extract

2 cups fresh berries (blueberries, strawberries, raspberries, blackberries, or a mixture)

2 tablespoons chopped fresh mint, for garnish (optional)

1. Open the can of coconut milk without shaking it and scoop out the thickened coconut cream from the top into a medium bowl, reserving the water for drinking or a smoothie.

2. Add the vanilla and whisk until thickened.

3. To serve, divide half of the berries between two chilled beverage glasses.

4. Top with about 2 inches of the cream.

5. Add the remaining berries and top with the remaining cream.

6. Garnish with the mint (if using) and serve.

Nutrition Facts

Calorie 503 | Fats 48g | Carbs 22g | Protein 6g

Chocolate flavored Almond Ball

Preparation Time: 5 minutes | Cook time: 10 minutes | Servings 16

1½ cups raw almonds

½ cup creamy unsalted almond butter

¼ cup raw cacao powder

3 tablespoons coconut oil, melted

2 tablespoons raw honey or maple syrup

¼ teaspoon ground cinnamon

1. Place the nuts in a food processor and pulse until finely ground.

2. Add the remaining ingredients and pulse until a smooth, sticky dough forms, 1 to 2 minutes.

3. Scoop out 1 heaping tablespoon of dough at a time to form 1½-inch balls, placing them on an aluminum foil– or parchment paper–lined baking sheet or plate so they don't touch.

4. Refrigerate the truffles until firm, about 1 hour.

Nutrition Facts

Calorie 148 | Fats 12g | Carbs 7g | Protein 5g

Healthy Date Coconut Flake Cookies

Preparation Time: 5 minutes | Cook time: 15 minutes | Servings 12

1 cup chopped pitted dates

1 medium banana, peeled

1/4 teaspoon vanilla

13/4 cups unsweetened coconut flakes

1. Preheat oven to 375°F. Cover dates in water and soak for about 10 minutes until softened. Drain.

2. Process together dates, banana, and vanilla in a food processor until almost smooth. Stir in coconut flakes by hand until thick. You may need a little more or less than 13/4 cups.

3. Drop by generous tablespoonful onto a cookie sheet.

4. Bake for 10–12 minutes or until golden brown. Cookies will be soft and chewy.

Cinnamon Nutty Fruity Dessert

Preparation Time: 5 minutes | Cook time: 30 minutes | Servings 6

4 cups peeled, cored, sliced apples

1/2 cup sliced cranberries

1/3 cup maple syrup

2 tablespoons coconut oil

1 teaspoon ground cinnamon

1/4 teaspoon ground nutmeg

3/4 cup combined chopped walnuts and almonds

1. Combine all ingredients except nuts in a cooker.

2. Cover and cook on high for 30 minutes or until apples are tender.

3. Sprinkle each serving with nuts.

Walnut Coconut Chocolate Squares

Preparation Time: 5 minutes | Cook time: 0 minutes | Servings 16

1 cup finely chopped walnuts

1 cup unsweetened grated coconut

3 cups crushed "Graham" Crackers

2/3 cup canned full-fat coconut milk

14 ounces chopped dark chocolate

2 teaspoons vanilla

1. Grease a 9" square pan with coconut oil and set aside.

2. In a large bowl, combine walnuts, coconut, and cracker crumbs; set aside.

3. In medium saucepan, combine coconut milk and chocolate.

4. Melt over low heat, stirring frequently, until smooth. Stir in vanilla. Reserve 1/3 cup of this mixture.

5. Pour remaining chocolate mixture over crumb mixture and stir to coat.

6. Press crumb mixture into prepared pan and spread reserved chocolate over top.

7. Place in refrigerator until set; cut into eight squares to serve.

Raisin Walnut Cookies

Preparation Time: 5 minutes | Cook time: 15 minutes | Makes 48 squares

2 cups maple syrup

4 cups almond flour

1/2 teaspoon nutmeg

1/2 teaspoon ginger

1/2 cup dates, chopped

2 cups ground walnuts

1/2 cup raisins

1. Preheat oven to 350°F. Line two large baking sheets with parchment paper.

2. Warm maple syrup in a medium saucepan over low heat for 5 minutes and let cool slightly.

3. In a medium bowl, sift together flour, nutmeg, and ginger.

4. Add maple syrup and stir until well blended. Stir in dates, walnuts, and raisins.

5. Roll dough to 1/4" thick and cut into forty-eight squares.

6. Place squares on prepared baking sheets and bake for 10 minutes.

7. Remove and cool.

Measurement Conversion Chart

VOLUME EQUIVALENTS(DRY)

US STANDARD	METRIC (APPROXIMATE)
1/8 teaspoon	0.5 mL
1/4 teaspoon	1 mL
1/2 teaspoon	2 mL
3/4 teaspoon	4 mL
1 teaspoon	5 mL
1 tablespoon	15 mL
1/4 cup	59 mL
1/2 cup	118 mL
3/4 cup	177 mL
1 cup	235 mL
2 cups	475 mL
3 cups	700 mL
4 cups	1 L

VOLUME EQUIVALENTS(LIQUID)

US STANDARD	US STANDARD (OUNCES)	METRIC (APPROXIMATE)
2 tablespoons	1 fl.oz.	30 mL
1/4 cup	2 fl.oz.	60 mL
1/2 cup	4 fl.oz.	120 mL
1 cup	8 fl.oz.	240 mL
1 1/2 cup	12 fl.oz.	355 mL
2 cups or 1 pint	16 fl.oz.	475 mL
4 cups or 1 quart	32 fl.oz.	1 L
1 gallon	128 fl.oz.	4 L

TEMPERATURES EQUIVALENTS

FAHRENHEIT(F)	CELSIUS(C) (APPROXIMATE)
225 °F	107 °C
250 °F	120 °C
275 °F	135 °C
300 °F	150 °C
325 °F	160 °C
350 °F	180 °C
375 °F	190 °C
400 °F	205 °C
425 °F	220 °C
450 °F	235 °C
475 °F	245 °C
500 °F	260 °C

WEIGHT EQUIVALENTS

US STANDARD	METRIC (APPROXIMATE)
1 ounce	28 g
2 ounces	57 g
5 ounces	142 g
10 ounces	284 g
15 ounces	425 g
16 ounces (1 pound)	455 g
1.5 pounds	680 g
2 pounds	907 g

CPSIA information can be obtained
at www.ICGtesting.com
Printed in the USA
LVHW051654010621
689062LV00009B/576

9 781802 838169